This book was compiled by Daniel Melehi
with the A.I assistance of Inventabot

Dedication

I hope this helps all of my wonderful
readers achieve all their goals in their
business. And I would like to thank my
wonderful wife for all of her continued
support in all my ventures.

Contents

Introduction

Welcome to "Entrepreneurial Mindset: How to Think and Act Like a Successful Business Owner," a comprehensive guide to developing the mindset necessary for becoming a successful entrepreneur. In this book, we will explore the characteristics of an entrepreneurial mindset, the importance of developing it, and steps to build a foundation for success. We will cover taking action and developing a plan, building relationships, managing finances, embracing change, and the importance of self-care and reflection. By the end of this book, you will have a deeper understanding of what it takes to succeed as an entrepreneur and how to develop the skills necessary to do so. A successful entrepreneurial mindset is not only beneficial for starting a business, but it is also essential for success in any aspect of life. So, whether you are an aspiring entrepreneur, small business owner, or just looking to improve your mindset, this book is for you. Let's get started! Understanding the Entrepreneurial Mindset: Having an entrepreneurial mindset means having a way of thinking that enables you to come up with new ideas, identify opportunities, and take risks. This mindset is not limited to business owners and entrepreneurs but can be developed by anyone who wants to succeed in any area of life. To develop an entrepreneurial mindset, you need to have certain characteristics such as creativity, resilience, and adaptability. You also need to cultivate a mindset that embraces challenges and failure as opportunities for growth and development. In this chapter, we will delve deeper into understanding the entrepreneurial mindset and how it can be cultivated in individuals. We will explore the characteristics that make up an entrepreneurial mindset and why it is important to develop this way of thinking in today's world.

CHARACTERISTICS OF AN ENTREPRENEURIAL MINDSET

Developing an entrepreneurial mindset is essential to achieving success in the world of business. However, it's not just about having a good idea or being able to take risks. It's about cultivating a particular set of skills and attitudes that allow you to think and act like a successful business owner. Here are some of the most crucial characteristics of an entrepreneurial mindset:

Creativity and Innovation

Entrepreneurs are often lauded for their creativity and innovation. They are not afraid to think outside of the box and come up with new and original solutions to problems. They also understand that innovation is not just about creating something completely new but also about finding ways to improve existing products or services.

Risk-taking

Another important characteristic of entrepreneurship is risk-taking. Entrepreneurs are willing to take calculated risks to pursue their business ideas, even if there is no guarantee of success. They understand that failure is a possibility but are not afraid of it. Instead, they use it as a learning experience to improve and refine their strategies.

Customer-focus

Entrepreneurs are acutely aware of the importance of the customer. They understand that without customers, their businesses would not exist. As such, they prioritize making their customers happy and meeting their needs. They are also adept at anticipating customer needs and adjusting their products or services accordingly.

Perseverance

Building a successful business is not easy, and entrepreneurs know it. They understand that setbacks and failures are an inevitable part of the process. However, they also possess the perseverance and resilience to push through those challenges and keep working towards their goals. By cultivating these characteristics, aspiring entrepreneurs can develop the necessary mindset to build successful businesses. However, developing an entrepreneurial mindset is only one part of the puzzle. In the next subchapter, we will delve into why developing an entrepreneurial mindset is so crucial in the first place.

THE IMPORTANCE OF DEVELOPING ENTREPRENEURIAL MINDSET

Developing an entrepreneurial mindset is vital for anyone who wants to start and run a successful business. It's not enough to have a great idea; you need to have the skills and mindset to turn that idea into a reality. One of the most important benefits of developing an entrepreneurial mindset is the ability to think creatively and identify opportunities that others may overlook. This is particularly valuable in today's fast-paced business environment, where innovation and agility are key to staying ahead of the competition. In addition, developing an entrepreneurial mindset can help you become more resilient and adaptable. As a business owner, you will inevitably face setbacks and challenges, and the ability to bounce back quickly and adjust your approach is essential. Another key benefit of developing an entrepreneurial mindset is the ability to take calculated risks. While many people are understandably risk-averse, successful entrepreneurs know that taking calculated risks can be the key to achieving success. The ability to evaluate risk, mitigate it, and move forward despite the potential for failure is a hallmark of a successful entrepreneurial mindset.

Ultimately, developing an entrepreneurial mindset is about embracing a growth mindset and continuously seeking new opportunities for learning and growth. It's a mindset that values creativity, innovation, and adaptability and is crucial for anyone who wants to succeed as a business owner.

Building a Strong Foundation

Starting a business requires a solid foundation if you want to succeed in the long run. This chapter is all about identifying and establishing the crucial elements of your enterprise. These essential elements include your core values and beliefs, as well as clarifying your vision and your goals.

IDENTIFYING YOUR CORE VALUES AND BELIEFS

Your core values and beliefs represent your fundamental principles and guide your decisions and actions. These are the values that you hold dear to your heart and that you apply in every aspect of your life, including your business. Taking time to identify and understand your core values and beliefs is an excellent place to start in building a strong foundation for your enterprise. Once you've identified your values, you need to make sure that they are ingrained in the DNA of your business. This means promoting them within your team and demonstrating them to your customers through your service or product offerings.

CLARIFYING YOUR VISION AND GOALS

Knowing what you want to achieve is essential as you embark on building your business. Your vision provides the direction for your enterprise, and your goals establish the milestones that you'll need to hit to get there. Being specific about what you want is crucial. It enables you to focus your attention effectively and direct your resources and energies more efficiently. Creating clear and measurable goals is a crucial step in building a foundation for your business. They provide a roadmap that outlines your progress and helps you stay on track towards achieving your vision. By setting realistic timelines and ensuring that your goals align with your values, you'll increase the chances of achieving them. Remember, your business's vision and goals should reflect your values and beliefs. By setting them in stone, you establish certainty and a path forward that enhances your probability of success.

SUBCHAPTER 3.1: IDENTIFYING YOUR CORE VALUES AND BELIEFS

As an entrepreneur, it's important to have a clear understanding of your core values and beliefs because they will guide your decision making and help you stay true to yourself and your goals. Your values are the fundamental beliefs that are most important to you, while your beliefs are thoughts and convictions that you hold to be true. To identify your core values, take some time to reflect on what matters most to you. Ask yourself questions such as "What do I stand for? What principles do I strive to live by? What makes me feel fulfilled and happy?" Write down your answers and look for patterns or themes. Once you have identified your core values, it's important to align your business decisions with them. This will ensure that you are building a business that is true to yourself and your values. For example, if one of your core values is environmentalism, you may want to ensure that your business practices are environmentally conscious. Identifying your beliefs is also important because they can impact your mindset and your approach to challenges and opportunities in your business. Take some time to examine your beliefs by asking yourself questions such as "What do I believe about success and failure? What do I believe about taking risks?" By understanding your core values and beliefs, you'll have a clearer sense of who you are and what you stand for. This will allow you to build a business that is true to yourself and your principles, making it more likely that you will find success and fulfillment.

CLARIFYING YOUR VISION AND GOALS

As an entrepreneur, it is crucial to have a clear understanding of your vision and goals. Your vision is your big picture, what you ultimately want to achieve with your business. Your goals are the specific, measurable steps you will take to bring your vision to life. Clarifying your vision and goals is essential because it gives you direction and helps you stay focused. Without a clear vision and goals, it is easy to get sidetracked, and your business may not reach its full potential. To clarify your vision, start by asking yourself questions about what you want your business to achieve in the long term. Consider your values, passions, and strengths. What problem do you want to solve, and what impact do you want to make on the world? Write a statement that reflects your ultimate goal and vision for your business. Your vision statement should be inspiring and guide your decisions. Once you have a clear vision, it is time to set goals that will bring it to life. Your goals should be specific, measurable, achievable, relevant, and time-bound. Consider breaking down your long-term vision into shorter-term goals that you can accomplish in the next few months or years. Track your progress toward your goals and make adjustments as necessary. Remember, your vision and goals may evolve over time as your business grows and changes. Be flexible and willing to adapt your plans to meet new challenges and opportunities. With a clear vision and well-defined goals, you can stay focused on the big picture and make progress toward achieving your entrepreneurial dreams.

Chapter 4: Taking Action

Taking action is a crucial aspect of the entrepreneurial mindset. It's not enough to dream, plan, and hope for success; you have to take action to make it happen. In this chapter, we'll discuss how to develop a solid plan of action, how to overcome obstacles that may hinder your progress, and how to persevere through challenging times.

SUBCHAPTER 4.1: DEVELOPING YOUR PLAN OF ACTION

A plan of action is a roadmap that helps you navigate the journey to success. It's crucial to have a well thought-out plan that outlines your goals, strategies, and milestones. Here are a few tips to help you create your plan:

1. Define your goals:

Start by identifying your top priorities and long-term goals. Write them down and be specific about what you want to achieve.

2. Break it down:

Once you've identified your main goals, break them down into smaller, more manageable steps. This will help you stay organized and give you a clear idea of what needs to be done.

3. Create a timeline:

Set specific deadlines for each step, so you stay on track and focused.

4. Identify your resources:

Determine what resources you need to accomplish your goals, such as funding, personnel, and technology.

5. Monitor and adjust:

Continuously evaluate your progress and adjust your plan as necessary. Be flexible and open to change.

SUBCHAPTER 4.2: OVERCOMING OBSTACLES AND PERSEVERING

No matter how great your plan is, obstacles and challenges are inevitable. It's how you respond to these obstacles that will determine your success. Here are a few tips to help you overcome and persevere:

1. Stay focused on your goals:

Keep your eye on the prize and remember why you started this journey. Don't lose sight of your ultimate goal.

2. Stay positive:

It's easy to get discouraged when things don't go as planned, but maintaining a positive attitude can help you get through difficult times.

3. Be resourceful:

Think outside the box and come up with creative solutions to problems.

4. Network and collaborate:

Sometimes, you need the help of others to overcome obstacles. Network and collaborate with like-minded individuals who can offer support and guidance.

5. Persevere:

Success rarely comes easy. It takes hard work, determination, and perseverance to overcome challenges and achieve your goals. Remember, taking action is only the first step towards success. Keep pushing forward, stay focused on your goals, and be open to new opportunities and challenges along the way.

DEVELOPING YOUR PLAN OF ACTION

An essential characteristic of successful entrepreneurs is their ability to plan effectively. Without a clear plan of action, it can be challenging to stay on track and achieve your objectives. The first step in creating a plan of action is to identify your goals and objectives. What do you want to achieve, and why is it important to you? Be specific and measurable when setting your goals, and don't be afraid to break them down into smaller milestones for easier tracking. Once you have your goals in place, it's time to start brainstorming ideas and strategies for achieving them. Get creative and think outside the box! Don't be afraid to take risks and try new approaches. Remember, innovation is a key trait of successful entrepreneurs. Once you have a list of potential strategies, it's important to evaluate each one carefully. Consider the potential risks and rewards, and assess which strategies align best with your values and goals. It's also a good idea to seek feedback and advice from trusted mentors and colleagues. Once you have a solid plan of action, it's important to stay organized and focused on your goals. Set deadlines and track your progress regularly to ensure you are on track to achieve your objectives. And remember, a plan of action is not set in stone – be open to making adjustments and changes as needed to stay agile and responsive to changing circumstances.

SUBCHAPTER 4.2: OVERCOMING OBSTACLES AND PERSEVERING

As an entrepreneur, you will undoubtedly face obstacles that challenge your business success. These obstacles can come in various forms, such as financial, logistical, or personal challenges. However, it is essential to understand that overcoming these obstacles is part of the entrepreneurial journey. It is the perseverance and resilience that distinguish successful entrepreneurs from others. One of the first steps in overcoming obstacles is to have a positive mindset. You must believe in your ability to handle any challenge and find solutions that work for you. Do not let fear or doubt cloud your judgment, and do not be afraid to seek help or advice from mentors or experts. Another important aspect of overcoming obstacles is to have a plan in place. Before starting your business, you should have a clear understanding of potential challenges and how you will address them. This plan should include contingency measures that you can implement if your original plan does not work as expected. It is also crucial to be adaptable and flexible when facing obstacles. Sometimes, unexpected challenges arise that require you to adjust your business plan or strategy. Successful entrepreneurs are those who can pivot and make changes quickly without losing sight of their overall goals. Remember that setbacks and failures are opportunities to learn and grow. Use each challenge as a learning experience, and let it inspire you to do better moving forward. Perseverance is key to success, and the ability to bounce back from adversity will serve you well in your entrepreneurial journey. In conclusion, overcoming obstacles and persevering is an essential part of the entrepreneurial mindset. Believe in yourself, have a plan in place, be adaptable and flexible, and see each challenge as an opportunity to learn and grow. With perseverance and resilience, you can overcome any obstacle and achieve your business goals.

Building Relationships

In order to be successful in business, it's important to build strong relationships with others. This includes networking with other professionals, collaborating with colleagues, and effectively communicating with clients and customers.

NETWORKING AND COLLABORATING

Networking is an essential part of building relationships in business. Connecting with other professionals in your industry can lead to new opportunities, partnerships, and valuable insights. Attending industry events, joining professional organizations, and utilizing social media platforms can all be effective ways to expand your network. Collaborating with colleagues can also aid in building strong relationships. Working together on projects and combining skill sets can lead to more successful outcomes and also foster a sense of camaraderie in the workplace.

Communicating Effectively

Effective communication is key to building strong relationships with clients and customers. This includes active listening, clear and concise language, and responsiveness. It's important to establish open lines of communication and be transparent and honest in all interactions. This can lead to greater trust and loyalty from clients and customers. Overall, building relationships is an integral part of being a successful business owner. By networking, collaborating, and communicating effectively, you can establish a strong foundation of trust and support within your industry.

NETWORKING AND COLLABORATING

Networking and collaborating are essential parts of building a successful business. By building strong relationships with other entrepreneurs and business leaders, you can gain valuable insights, access resources, and create partnerships that can enhance your business. To begin networking, it's important to attend events, conferences, and workshops specifically geared towards entrepreneurs. This gives you the chance to meet others who share similar interests, goals, and challenges. It also allows you to learn about the latest industry trends, technologies, and strategies. When attending networking events, make sure to bring business cards and be prepared to talk about your business and what makes it unique. It's also important to be a good listener and to ask questions of others. This can help you build meaningful connections and gain valuable insights. Collaborating with other entrepreneurs can also be an effective way to grow your business. By joining forces with others, you can pool resources, share knowledge, and tap into new networks and markets. To identify potential collaborators, look for entrepreneurs who share your values, have complementary skills, and target similar audiences. When approaching potential collaborators, make sure to clearly articulate your vision and goals for the collaboration. It's also important to be open to different ideas and to communicate effectively to ensure everyone is on the same page. Remember, networking and collaboration should be a two-way street. By providing value to others and building a strong reputation, you can create a network of supporters who are invested in your success.

SUBCHAPTER 5.2: COMMUNICATING EFFECTIVELY

Effective communication is a crucial skill to have as an entrepreneur. It involves transmitting your ideas, opinions, and messages clearly and concisely to others. As a business owner, you will need to communicate with a variety of people, including employees, customers, investors, and suppliers. Therefore, honing your communication skills is vital for building strong relationships and growing your business. One key aspect of effective communication is active listening. This means paying attention to what the other person is saying, asking questions, and clarifying any misunderstandings. It also involves being empathetic and understanding the other person's perspective. These skills will help you to connect with people on a deeper level and build trust. Another crucial component of effective communication is choosing the right medium. Depending on the situation, you may need to communicate in person, over the phone, via email, or through social media. Each of these mediums has its own strengths and weaknesses, and selecting the appropriate one can help ensure that your message is received and understood. Finally, when communicating, it's important to be concise, clear, and confident. Avoid using jargon or complex terminology that others may not understand. Instead, try to explain your ideas in simple language that anyone can comprehend. Also, be confident when delivering your message. Speak clearly and with conviction, and always be prepared to answer any questions or concerns that may arise. In summary, effective communication skills are essential for entrepreneurs. By actively listening, choosing the right medium, and being concise and confident when delivering your message, you can build strong relationships and take your business to new heights.

Chapter 6: Managing Your Finances

As an entrepreneur, managing your finances is crucial to the success of your business. In this chapter, we will explore the key concepts you need to understand to keep your finances in order.

SUBCHAPTER 6.1: UNDERSTANDING CASH FLOW

Cash flow is the lifeblood of your business. It refers to the movement of money in and out of your business and is essential to maintain good financial health. Understanding your cash flow is crucial to ensure that you have a clear picture of your business's financial situation. One of the essential tools for managing your cash flow is a cash flow statement. This statement shows the inflow and outflow of cash over a specific period. By analyzing your cash flow statement, you can identify any cash gaps and address them before they become a problem.

SUBCHAPTER 6.2: BUDGETING AND SAVING

Another critical aspect of financial management is budgeting and saving. A budget is a plan that outlines your expected income and expenses for a particular period. By creating a budget, you can track your spending, identify areas where you can cut costs and plan for future expenses. Creating a savings plan is also an essential part of financial management. By putting aside a portion of your income each month, you can build an emergency fund and invest in the future growth of your business.

To Sum Up

In summary, managing your finances is critical to the success of your business. By understanding your cash flow, creating a budget, and saving for the future, you can keep your business on track and ensure long-term financial stability. In the next chapter, we will discuss the importance of innovation and embracing change as an entrepreneur.

UNDERSTANDING CASH FLOW

Cash flow is the lifeblood of any business. It's the money that goes in and out of your business, and it's the key to understanding the financial health of your company. If your business has more cash coming in than going out, you have positive cash flow. If you have more money going out than coming in, you have negative cash flow. Understanding your cash flow is critical to the success of your business. It allows you to see where your money is coming from and where it's going. It can help you anticipate cash shortages and plan for the future. There are two main components of cash flow: cash inflows and cash outflows. Cash inflows are the money coming into your business from sales, investments, and other sources. Cash outflows are the money going out, such as expenses, salaries, and payments on loans. To manage your cash flow effectively, you need to monitor your cash inflows and outflows carefully. You should keep track of your accounts receivable (money owed to you), your accounts payable (what you owe to others), and your cash reserves. It's also a good idea to develop a cash flow projection. This is an estimate of your expected cash inflows and outflows over a given period of time. A cash flow projection can help you plan for unexpected expenses, slow periods, or other issues that could affect your cash flow. By understanding and managing your cash flow, you can avoid cash shortages, make smart financial decisions, and ensure the long-term success of your business. So take the time to review your cash flow regularly and make adjustments as needed. Your business will thank you for it. As an entrepreneur, it's crucial to understand the importance of managing your finances and developing a comprehensive budget plan. By creating a budget, you can track and manage your expenses, monitor your cash flow, and ensure that you're making sound financial decisions. The first step in creating a budget is to identify your business's fixed and variable expenses. Fixed expenses are those that don't change from month to month, such as rent, insurance, and salaries. Variable expenses are those that fluctuate based on your business's activity, like raw materials, advertising, and equipment maintenance. Once you have identified your expenses, you can start to set financial goals for your business. These goals could include increasing revenue, lowering expenses, or saving for future investments. To achieve these goals, you'll need to create a detailed budget plan that considers all of your expenses and income streams. You may want to consider using budgeting software or working with a financial advisor to help you develop a comprehensive budget plan that works for your unique needs. In addition to budgeting, it's also important to prioritize saving as an entrepreneur. By saving regularly, you can build up an emergency fund, invest in future business opportunities, or even pay down debt. Some effective strategies for saving as an entrepreneur include setting up automatic contributions to a savings account, taking advantage of tax incentives for retirement savings, and negotiating with suppliers for better prices. With budgeting and saving as priorities in your business, you can ensure that your finances stay on track and that your business has a solid financial foundation for future success.

Chapter 7: Innovating and Embracing Change

Innovation is the lifeblood of entrepreneurship. The world is constantly changing, and it's essential to stay ahead of the curve to succeed. As an entrepreneur, you should embrace change and be willing to take risks to stay relevant and competitive.

SUBCHAPTER 7.1: STAYING AHEAD OF THE CURVE

To stay ahead of the curve, you must continually monitor trends in your industry and adapt your business accordingly. Look for opportunities to innovate and stay on top of emerging technologies. This may involve investing in new equipment, software, or processes. Don't be afraid to try something new and experiment with different approaches.

Technology

Technology is a driving force behind innovation and change. As an entrepreneur, it's critical to stay up-to-date with the latest technological advancements and be willing to integrate them into your business. Embracing technology can improve efficiency, reduce costs, and increase revenue.

Research and Development

Research and development (R&D) is essential for driving innovation. By investing in R&D, you can develop new products, services, and processes that set you apart from your competitors. This may involve testing and refining your ideas to ensure they are viable and marketable.

SUBCHAPTER 7.2: EMBRACING RISK AND FAILURE

Innovation and change involve risk, and failure is a natural part of the process. As an entrepreneur, you need to be comfortable taking risks and willing to learn from your mistakes. Don't be afraid to try something new, even if it's outside of your comfort zone.

Risk Management

While risk is an inherent part of entrepreneurship, it's important to manage it effectively. This may involve conducting risk assessments and developing contingency plans to mitigate potential losses.

Learning from Failure

Failure is inevitable, but it's also an opportunity to learn and grow. Instead of dwelling on your mistakes, focus on the lessons you can take away from them. Take the time to reflect on what went wrong and develop a plan for how you can improve in the future. Remember, every successful entrepreneur has faced failure at some point in their journey. In conclusion, innovation and change are essential for entrepreneurial success. By staying ahead of the curve and embracing risk and failure, you can create a thriving business that's prepared for the future.

STAYING AHEAD OF THE CURVE

In today's fast-changing business world, it's essential for entrepreneurs to stay ahead of the curve. This means constantly innovating and updating your products and services to meet the changing needs of your customers. One way to stay ahead of the curve is to keep up with industry trends and advancements in technology. This can be done by attending industry events and conferences, reading trade publications, and networking with other business owners. Another important aspect of staying ahead of the curve is to be open to feedback and willing to adapt. Listening to your customers' feedback and making changes based on their needs is essential for long-term success. Finally, it's important to have a growth mindset and be willing to take calculated risks. This may involve investing in new technologies or exploring new markets. By embracing change and taking calculated risks, you can set your business up for long-term success.

EMBRACING RISK AND FAILURE

One of the distinguishing features of successful entrepreneurs is their willingness to take risks. They understand that failure is an inevitable part of the journey, and they see it as an opportunity to learn and grow. It's important to embrace risk and view it as an opportunity rather than a threat. Being risk-averse may feel safe, but it also limits your potential for growth and success. By taking calculated risks, you open yourself up to new opportunities and experiences that can help you achieve your goals. Furthermore, failure shouldn't be feared but embraced. While it may be initially discouraging, it can provide valuable lessons for future endeavors. It's important to see every failure as an opportunity to learn and grow. By embracing failure, you shift your mindset from one of defeat to one of growth and development. It's important to understand that not every risk you take will lead to success. However, it's only through trying and failing that you can ultimately achieve success. With each failure, you gain experience, resilience, and a deeper understanding of what does and doesn't work. As an entrepreneur, it's crucial to develop a growth mindset and view failure as a necessary part of the journey. By embracing risk and failure, you position yourself for success in the long run.

Chapter 8: The Importance of Self-Care and Reflection

As an entrepreneur, it's easy to get caught up in the hustle and bustle of everyday business operations. However, it's important to take a step back and focus on yourself as well. In this chapter, we'll discuss the importance of self-care and reflection in maintaining a healthy entrepreneurial mindset.

SUBCHAPTER 8.1: BALANCING WORK AND LIFE

Maintaining a healthy work-life balance is crucial for any entrepreneur. Overworking yourself can lead to burnout, which can ultimately hurt your business in the long run. It's important to prioritize self-care activities, such as exercise, meditation, and spending time with loved ones. One effective strategy for balancing work and life is to establish boundaries and stick to them. Set specific times for work and for leisure, and make sure to separate the two as much as possible. This could mean turning off your work phone after a certain time each day, or committing to taking one day off per week to recharge.

SUBCHAPTER 8.2: PRACTICING MINDFULNESS AND GRATITUDE

In addition to balancing work and life, practicing mindfulness and gratitude can also have a positive impact on your entrepreneurial mindset. Mindfulness involves being present in the moment and fully engaged in what you're doing, without judgment or distraction. This can help reduce stress and improve focus. Gratitude involves being thankful for the people and things in your life. By taking a few moments each day to reflect on what you're grateful for, you can shift your focus away from stress and negativity and towards positivity and abundance. This can lead to a more optimistic and inspired outlook on your business and your life. In summary, prioritizing self-care and reflection can help you maintain a strong and healthy entrepreneurial mindset. By balancing work and life, practicing mindfulness, and cultivating gratitude, you can stay focused, motivated, and ultimately more successful in your business endeavors.

BALANCING WORK AND LIFE

One of the biggest challenges in being a successful entrepreneur is finding a way to balance work and life. It can be challenging to manage the demands of starting and running a successful business while also taking care of yourself and your loved ones. However, achieving a healthy work-life balance is essential for preventing burnout and maintaining your mental health and well-being. There are several strategies you can use to help balance work and life as an entrepreneur. One important strategy is to prioritize your time and set boundaries around your work. This means making sure you have set work hours and sticking to them, even when you have a lot of tasks to complete. It also means taking breaks throughout the day and making time for personal activities that help you relax and recharge. Another important strategy is to learn to delegate effectively. As an entrepreneur, it can be tempting to try and do everything yourself, but this can quickly lead to burnout and decreased productivity. Instead, identify the tasks that are most important for you to do and delegate the rest to trusted employees or freelancers. Finally, it's important to communicate your needs and boundaries to those around you. This means letting your clients, employees, and loved ones know when you are available and when you need to take time off. By being open and honest about your needs, you can help prevent misunderstandings and ensure that everyone is on the same page. Remember, achieving a healthy work-life balance is an ongoing process, and it takes time and practice to get it right. By prioritizing your time, delegating effectively, and communicating your needs, you can find a way to balance work and life and achieve success as an entrepreneur.

PRACTICING MINDFULNESS AND GRATITUDE

As an entrepreneur, it's easy to get caught up in the hustle and bustle of everyday life. It's important, however, to take a step back and practice mindfulness and gratitude. Mindfulness is the practice of being present in the moment and aware of one's thoughts and feelings. By practicing mindfulness, you can reduce stress and anxiety, increase focus and productivity, and improve overall well-being. Gratitude is the practice of acknowledging and appreciating the good things in life. By practicing gratitude, you can improve relationships, increase happiness, and reduce stress. As an entrepreneur, taking time to practice mindfulness and gratitude can have a profound impact on your success. By being mindful and grateful, you can cultivate a positive mindset, which can help you overcome challenges and achieve your goals. Some ways to practice mindfulness and gratitude include meditation, journaling, spending time in nature, and expressing gratitude to others. Try incorporating some of these practices into your daily routine and see how they can benefit you and your business.